Growing organic vegetables

Gardening **organically**

One of the great joys of gardening is to experience the variety of life that a healthy garden contains. A garden managed using organic methods will have far more interest in it than a garden where insecticides and chemicals are used. An organic garden is a more balanced environment, where 'good' creatures such as ladybirds and beetles keep the 'bad' pests and diseases under control.

Organically grown plants also tend to be healthier and stronger than plants that rely on large doses of artificial fertiliser. In healthy soil they grow strong roots and can better withstand attack by pests and diseases. Soil can be kept in top condition by recycling garden waste to make nutritious compost. Growing the right combination of plants in the right place at the right time – by rotating where you plant your veg for example, or choosing shrubs to suit the growing conditions that your garden can offer – can deliver impressive disease-free results.

These are the basic principles of organic growing – use the natural resources you already have to create a balanced and vibrant garden. It's sustainable, cheaper than buying chemicals, easier than you think and great fun. Enjoy your organic gardening.

Nothing beats the taste of freshly picked, vitamin packed, organic vegetables – particularly when there is the added satisfaction of knowing you grew them yourself without using pesticides or chemical fertilisers.

Contrary to what many people think, you don't need a large garden, or a lot of time or expertise to start growing vegetables. You can grow them without digging and you can even grow them in pots. The trick is to start small, with just a few choice crops and take it from there. This book will get you started but, be warned; once you start you may never stop!

Contents

What you could soon be eating from your garden   **7**
Choosing what to grow   8
Local climate   9
What will be available and when?   14
10 good reasons for growing your own organic vegetables   16

Getting started   **17**
What do you need to grow vegetables?   18
Veg talk – what does it all mean?   22
Preparing the ground for vegetables   24
Feeding the soil   27
Starting the vegetables   33
Sowing direct into the soil   34
Raising young plants   38

Growing methods   **45**
Growing in beds   46
Vegetables without digging   47
Growing in containers   50
Vegetable families   52

Maintenance   **55**
Mulching   58

Resources   **63**

1

What you could soon be eating from your garden

Choosing **what to grow**

What do you like to eat?

You might like to grow vegetables that tend to be disappointing or expensive when bought from the shops (runner beans, peas, tomatoes or sprouting broccoli for example) or vegetables that are difficult to buy (kohl rabi or purple skinned potatoes for example). The fact that they're hard to find or expensive to buy doesn't necessarily mean they're hard to grow.

Send for some mail order seed catalogues including the specialist organic seed suppliers, to give you an idea of the huge diversity that we can grow in the UK. Then check out the factors on the following pages that will help narrow down your choice.

Local **climate**

Some vegetables, such as carrots, leeks, onions, parsnips and broad beans, are hardy. They don't much mind the British weather, and will grow well in most parts of the country.

Other crops are more tender. They need warm soil and weather to grow well, and won't withstand the frost. These include sweetcorn, courgettes and some tomatoes.

Really tender vegetables, including peppers, aubergines and some tomatoes need a really warm sheltered location to thrive outdoors, and are only suitable for growing in a greenhouse in many areas.

Sun or **shade?**

Vegetables do best in a spot that gets full light all day or for at least 6 hours. Beetroot, calabrese, chicory, endive, kale, lettuce, peas, spinach, radish and jerusalem artichoke will tolerate light shade in summer.

Quick returns

Seed to crop in 5* weeks or less – radish, loose leaf lettuce, rocket, spinach, pak choi.

Seed to crop in 10* weeks or less – spring onions, kohl rabi, florence fennel, chinese cabbage, chard, dwarf french beans, early carrots, baby beetroot.

*exact timing will vary with sowing time and climate

These vegetables can be sown several times through the spring and summer to give a continuous supply. This is known as successional sowing.

Lots of pickings from one plant

Runner beans, french beans, courgettes, loose leaf lettuce, spinach beet, chard, mangetout peas and tomatoes all produce continually.

You can make a first cut of salad leaves just a few weeks after sowing.

Easy **to grow?**

How easy a vegetable is to grow really depends on soil type, location, local pests and how keen you are – so everyone's list tends to be different. It's best just to get started and find out what suits you and your garden.

Vegetables that should be relatively simple to grow:

Potatoes, jerusalem artichokes, broad beans, french* and runner* beans, spinach beet, chard, onions from sets, garlic, salad bowl lettuce, courgettes*, pumpkins* and bush tomatoes*.

*even easier if you buy plants rather than raising your own

Unusual veg and varieties

It's fun to grow crops and varieties that you don't often (or ever) see in the shops. The gardener has a much wider choice than the greengrocer and many of these are really attractive and will enhance the look of any garden.

Why not try: Kohl rabi, scorzonera, rainbow chard, yellow and pink tomatoes, red frilly lettuces, purple leeks, purple skinned potatoes or yellow french beans.

Courgette plants are prolific providers.

11

With the right soil and plenty of sun, you could be eating beans like this for months.

Growing **upwards**

Climbing and trailing vegetables can be trained up a support, so they need little ground space to grow.

Grow up a wigwam or double row of canes
Runner beans and climbing french beans

Grow up netting or trellis
Peas, cucumbers, pumpkins and marrows

Seedling **salads** and **stir fries**

Many leafy vegetables can be cut when young to produce the quickest crop of leaves for salads and stir fries. Cut the young plants down when 3-6 weeks old, leaving a 5cm stump. This will re-grow to produce a second, or even third, crop.

Ideal for growing in wide containers such as seed trays, growing bags and also direct in the soil.

Sow seeds (approx 2.5cm apart) or plant out module raised plants as close as you can. Choose a mix of vegetables to suit your taste.

Some suitable vegetables for seedling salads and stir fries

Chard	*Chicory*
Chinese cabbage	*Endive*
Lettuce (non hearting)	*Kale*
Oriental greens	*Pak choi*
Radish leaves	*Rocket*
Spinach	

You can buy seed in ready mixed packets – 'saladini' for summer and autumn salads; 'oriental saladini' for salads and stir fries.

Sow seeds or plant out small plants grown in module pots as close as you can.

Chard and kale can be cut when young for seedling salads and stir fries.

What will be available **and when**?

Vegetable	Spring			Summer			Autumn				Winter	
	Mr	Ap	Ma	Ju	Jl	Au	S	O	N	D	J	F
Seedling crops	Y	Y	Y	Y	Y	Y	Y	Y	Y			
Beetroot*				Y	Y	Y	Y	Y				
Broad beans			Y	Y	Y	Y						
Broccoli, purple sprouting	Y	Y	Y								Y	Y
Bulb onions*				Y	Y	Y	Y					
Calabrese				Y	Y	Y	Y					
Carrots*				Y	Y	Y	Y	Y	Y	Y	Y	Y
Chard & Leaf beet	Y	Y	Y	Y	Y	Y	Y	Y	Y	Y	Y	Y
Chicory, red	Y					Y	Y	Y	Y	Y	Y	Y
Chinese cabbage							Y	Y	Y	Y		
Courgette				Y	Y	Y	Y	Y				
Endive	Y	Y	Y	Y	Y	Y	Y	Y	Y	Y	Y	Y
Florence fennel				Y	Y	Y	Y	Y				
French beans				Y	Y	Y	Y	Y				
Garlic*					Y	Y						
Kale	Y							Y	Y	Y	Y	Y
Kohl rabi,				Y	Y	Y	Y	Y				
Leeks	Y	Y					Y	Y	Y	Y	Y	Y
Lettuce, summer				Y	Y	Y	Y	Y				
Peas				Y	Y	Y	Y	Y				
Pak choi,							Y	Y	Y	Y	Y	
Parsnips*	Y						Y	Y	Y	Y	Y	Y
Peppers, sweet + chilli						Y	Y					
Potatoes*				Y	Y	Y	Y					
Radish, Summer												
Runner beans					Y	Y	Y					
Spinach	Y	Y	Y	Y	Y	Y	Y	Y	Y	Y	Y	Y
Spring onions			Y	Y	Y	Y	Y	Y				
Summer cabbage				Y	Y	Y	Y	Y				
Sweetcorn					Y	Y	Y	Y				
Tomatoes						Y	Y	Y				

*these crops can be stored to be eaten over a much longer period.
Many vegetables can also be frozen without loss of too much goodness or flavour.

10 good reasons for growing your own organic vegetables

1. The flavour of home grown veg is unbeatable

2. You'll know they are grown without pesticides

3. You can choose varieties that you never find in the shops

4. Fresh from the garden vegetables are top for nutritional value

5. Kids will learn where food really comes from

6. It's an activity the whole family can enjoy

7. It's fun and you can eat organic for less

8. It reconnects you with the seasons and seasonal eating

9. You can enjoy vegetables that are never at their best in the shops

10. Home grown is as local as you can get

2

Getting started

In a warm, sheltered spot you may even be able to grow peppers outside.

What do you need
for growing vegetables?

Light and sunshine

The best spot for growing vegetables is in an open, unshaded spot. Full light for at least 6 hours a day is essential for most crops. Some types of vegetable will tolerate light shade, especially in the summer. Try not to grow under trees.

Warmth and shelter

Tender crops such as tomatoes and peppers need a warm, sheltered spot. If you want to raise your own veg transplants (plants raised in pots and trays), you will need a sunny location protected from wind and rain.

A greenhouse or cloches can create warmth and shelter if the garden does not.

A windowsill with good light can be used to start young plants.

Water supply

Young plants will need to be watered. Once established most will only need watering in very dry weather and on quick draining soils. Vegetables in containers will need regular watering.

Collect rainwater (it's better for the plants) from the roof of your house or shed to use on everything except young seedlings in containers (which should be watered with tap water).

Soil

You may need to improve your soil or clear it of weeds before you can start to grow vegetables. Plants do not like waterlogged or heavy soils, or those that are compacted hard, or full of builders' rubble (see page 25).

Many vegetables can be grown in containers, but they generally need less care when grown in the ground.

A place to grow

Vegetables can be grown in their own plot (which can be as small as 1.25 sq m) or fitted in to an ornamental border. Some can be grown up a fence or canes to use vertical space. Don't grow next to a vigorous hedge or large shrubs as these will compete for food and water.

Basic **tools**

A fork, spade, rake, trowel and watering can are the basic necessities. A hoe is also useful.

Soil **improvers**

Compost, leafmould and other organic materials to maintain a healthy soil (see page 27).

Crop **covers**

It is useful to have a selection of crop covers, such as home-made bottle cloches and netting to hand to protect seedlings from cats, birds and the weather.

Organic **seeds and plants**

Organically grown seeds, seed potatoes, onion and garlic sets are available in many mail order seed catalogues. A more limited range of organically grown vegetable plants, for transplanting, are also available.

Some of the ingredients for success with vegetables.

Veg talk – what does it all mean?

Once you have chosen what vegetables to grow, next comes the choice of variety. The range available in seed catalogues is tremendous, but it can be a bit overwhelming. Here are some tips to help you decipher the jargon and make your choices:

'Early' – means quick to crop. Good for early sowings but also later ones too. Tend to be smaller than 'main crop' varieties, so good for containers and close planting.

For example: carrots, beetroot.

'Bush' – compact plant.
For example: tomato, cucumber, marrow, pumpkin.

'Trailing' – sprawling plant. May be trained to grow up a net or canes.
For example: cucumber, pumpkin, marrow.

'F1 hybrid' – modern hybrid bred to give vigorous, reliable crops. Designed, in the main, to crop all at once. Seed more expensive.

'Organic' – seed from plants grown under organic conditions.

'Date of introduction' – grow a bit of history. Quite a few favourite varieties were first introduced centuries ago, and are still worth growing today. Gardeners help to keep them in existence. Tend to suit small scale, garden style growing.

For example: Painted Lady runner bean (1855), Green Windsor broad bean (1809).

'Bolt resistant' or 'resistant to bolting' – some vegetables have a tendency to go straight to producing a flower stem before you've got a crop if sown at the wrong time. Bolt resistant varieties are much less fussy.

For example: beetroot, florence fennel.

'Pest (disease) resistant or tolerant' – the variety is less susceptible (though not immune) to the named pest or disease. A useful way of limiting damage if a particular pest or disease is a common problem.

For example: virus resistant courgettes, blight resistant potatoes.

Other varietal differences to consider include:

- Suitability of tender crops for growing outside rather than in a greenhouse

- Colour of stems, leaves, fruits and pods

- Suitability for different sowing times.

Fortunately, deep digging is not something you need to do often.

Preparing the ground for vegetables

To grow vegetables you need to create an area of weed free soil that is easy to fork over, that is free of large lumps of soil and that can be raked level. Plant roots need to be able to grow easily down into the soil, and tiny seedlings need to make their way up through it to the light.

If the ground has recently grown flowers or vegetables successfully, all you should need to do is remove any weeds.

Check underground

If you don't know the site, dig a hole or two (a spade or two deep) to see what is below the soil surface. If you find rubble and junk, dig it out. You may need to put in a quantity of your own compost to bring the level back up if there is a lot of rubbish to dig out.

If the ground is hard to dig, or has very solid layers, dig it over to break it up. Dig out a trench of soil a spade deep, then loosen the soil below using a fork. Repeat this across the area. It should only be necessary to do this level of preparation once.

Neglected **weedy ground**

If the area is small, simply fork it over and remove all traces of weeds and their roots by hand. You may need to do this several times.

For larger areas, it helps if you cover the ground with a sheet of black plastic. This needs to be well weighted down (use bricks, logs or soil filled plastic bags) to stop it blowing away. Gradually move the plastic back to reveal the next area to dig over. The black plastic prevents the weeds growing, and they will begin to die off. This makes digging easier.

Ripe for conversion. The soil just beneath the surface of a lawn is probably some of the best in your garden.

Unsightly though it is, if you leave the plastic in place for a year, all but the most persistent weeds will have gone.

Converting a lawn

The soil just beneath the surface of a lawn is probably some of the best in your garden so don't scrape off the turf and throw it away. For a small area, you can just dig it over, chopping up the turf as you go. Repeat the process a few times after a week or two to break up the turf and bury it in the soil.

Alternatively, cover the grass with a sheet of black plastic, or cardboard boxes topped with straw or grass mowings. Within a few months the site should be clear enough to start growing vegetables.

Feeding the soil

If the soil is in good condition, vegetables will thrive with little further attention – so it pays to look after your soil well and keep it healthy.

If you are starting out on a neglected or new plot with poor soil it may take a few years to get the soil up to scratch.

Acidity

The acidity (pH) of a soil affects how well plants grow. Most vegetables prefer a pH of around 6.5. You can measure the pH of your soil using a small kit which you can buy from garden centres. If the soil is too acid (the kit will tell you this) then add dolomite limestone to bring it to a pH of around 6.5. If it is too alkaline (limey), there is little you can do. If plants are already growing well in the garden there may be no need to bother with this test.

Never add lime if you don't know what the pH is.

Food and **fibre**

The way to build and maintain a good soil is to add bulky soil improvers such as home-made leafmould or compost and well rotted strawy manure. You can buy bagged soil improvers from garden centres or by mail order. Greenwaste compost – made from prunings from parks and other green waste that is taken to recycling sites – can be available cheaply from garden centres, composting sites or your local authority. Check with your local council.

All bulky soil improvers will help your vegetables to grow because they improve the structure or consistency of the soil. Using them will make heavy soils easier for plants to grow through, and they help dry soils hold more water.

Bulky soil improvers will help your vegetables to grow because they improve the structure or consistency of the soil.

Some - the 'richer soil improvers' on page 30 - also provide additional plant foods, that some vegetables require.

Dig soil improvers into the top few inches of soil, or spread over the soil surface (this is known as mulching).

Low nutrient **soil improvers**

Leafmould, fine grade bark

- Use where growing carrots, parsnips, fennel, celeriac, spinach, spinach beet, chard and anything else if you have plenty.
- Can be applied at any time of year.
- Apply as much as you like.

Municipal green waste compost

This compost is produced, in large scale composting plants, from the parks and gardens green waste that is collected from homes and recycling sites.

It is a good source of potassium and phosphate, so is particularly useful on fruiting crops such as tomatoes. The nitrogen it contains is very slow acting, so the compost can be applied at any time of year to any crops.

Use with a more nitrogen rich fertiliser or manure when growing the plants listed on the following pages (under richer soil improvers).

Apply 2-3 barrow loads per 5 sq m ground.

Richer soil improvers

Garden compost, well rotted manure, mushroom compost, purchased bagged manures and composts.

- Use where growing potatoes, tomatoes, leeks, cabbage, brussels sprouts, courgettes, pumpkins, sweetcorn.

- Also for most other crops (except carrots and parsnips) on poorer soils.

- Apply in spring and summer only.

- Garden compost – apply 2 barrow loads per 5 sq m of ground.

- Well rotted strawy manure – apply 1 barrow load per 5 sq m ground.

Fertilisers

Use fertilisers that are made from natural materials. They are slowly broken down in the soil to feed your vegetables. These fertilisers are useful on poor soils, and when you don't have enough compost or manure to feed all the plants that need it.

- Chicken manure pellets
- Potash of plant origin
- Blood, fish and bone meal - use mainly for propagating
- Blended general fertilisers
- Hoof and horn meal
- Seaweed meal from sustainable sources
- Rock phosphate

Plant and mineral based fertilisers are available for those who prefer to avoid animal based products.

Always use as directed on the packet.

Where possible, buy a certified product with a recognised organic logo such as that of the HDRA or the Soil Association.

Leeks can be sown direct outdoors into a nursery bed from March to early May. When the plants are 15cm or so tall, gently dig up them up and plant into their final cropping place.

Starting the vegetables

Most vegetables are grown from seed, sown either directly into the soil or into pots or trays in a warm place and planted out as young plants.

Some vegetables (see table on page 44) are planted as tubers, cloves or sets, rather than starting them from seed.

Most vegetables are sown or planted afresh after each crop. Depending on the crop, you either dig up the whole plant to eat it – carrots, hearting lettuces, parsnips for example. Or pick from it over a period of weeks, or even months – tomatoes, chard, courgettes, loose leaf lettuce and beans for example.

Sowing direct into the soil

Hardy crops (i.e those that don't mind frost and cool temperatures) can be sown directly into prepared ground where the vegetables are to grow to maturity. Some more tender crops can be direct sown once the soil has warmed up. The table on page 44 identifies which crops are suitable for direct sowing.

Seeds are usually sown in rows, but some are 'broadcast' over an area (see page 36).

Check page 44 and the seed packet to find out when the seeds can be sown. Soil and weather conditions, and your local climate will also have a bearing on sowing dates. There is no advantage in sowing too early when the soil is not warm enough to start them into growth.

Some more tender crops can be direct sown once the soil has warmed up. In most areas french beans may be sown direct between late April and late June.

Sowing direct step-by-step

1   Rake the ground level and relatively lump free.

2   Use a length of string between two sticks to mark the position of the row (or rows) to be sown.

3   Use the edge of a hoe, a rake, or a trowel to make a shallow trench along the length of the line. This is known as a 'drill'. Seed is usually sown at twice its own depth.

4   Water along the bottom of the drill.

5   Sow seed thinly (every inch or so) along the bottom of the drill, or sow a few seeds together at the final spacing distance suggested on the packet.

6   Rake soil back over the seeds and firm down gently. Label with variety name and sowing date.

7   Cover with netting if cats or birds are a problem, or with horticultural fleece for warmth early in the season.

Thin to avoid overcrowding

As the young seedlings grow, gently remove any that are crowding others, so that you end up with single plants at the required spacing (this should be noted on the packet). Water first if the ground is dry. You can eat the thinnings if they are big enough.

Nursery beds

Direct sowing is also used to raise cabbage, leeks, cauliflower, brussels sprouts and broccoli seedlings in an area of ground set aside as a 'nursery bed'. Sow seed in rows 15cm apart, with 3cm between seeds. When the plants are 15cm or so tall, gently dig up them up and plant into their final cropping place.

Broadcast sowing

Broadcast sowing is used for crops that need little space between plants. It is used particularly for cutting salads such as rocket, lettuce, oriental greens and chicory. It is also a useful technique for sowing spring onions and early carrots. Rake the ground level, then sprinkle seed evenly over the area, aiming to leave 2.5 cm or so between seeds. Gently rake the patch one way, and then at right angles, to cover the seed, or sieve some soil over it.

Planting **potatoes**

Buy organic seed potatoes a few weeks in advance of planting time. It can be convenient to set them in egg boxes. The upper end should be the one with a circle of tiny buds on it (known as the 'rose' end). Keep in a cool, light, frost free spot. Young shoots will grow from the tubers.

Plant out with the top of the potato 15cm below the surface, in trowel holes or a trench.

Spacing

Earlies: 30cm x 50cm

Main crops: 40cm x 75cm

Protect growing plants from frost.

Harvesting a crop of new 'no dig' potatoes.

Raising **young plants**

Plants raised in pots and trays – indoors on a light windowsill, or in a greenhouse or other suitably light spot - can be started off earlier than they could be sown outside, giving them a head start. Transplants are also useful where soil is not fine enough for direct sowing. It keeps them safe from slugs too. Buying young plants from a catalogue or garden centre is even easier. Carrots and parsnips are not suitable for starting this way. They must be sown direct.

Equipment needed

- Small pots (5-7.5cm across) – for tomatoes, courgettes marrows and pumpkins.

- Rootrainers – for runner beans, french beans, sweet corn.

- Divided trays (module trays) – for all other crops that can be transplanted (see page 44). If you buy bedding plants they often come in divided trays that can be used again for plant raising.

- Multipurpose compost – buy a peat free mix, soil or garden compost is too heavy and lumpy for seedlings.

The **process**

1 Fill pots or module trays to the top with moist multipurpose compost. Tap the sides to settle the compost, then firm it down gently.

2 Place seeds on the surface of the compost. If the seeds are small (eg lettuce, carrot or onion), sow 2 or 3 in each pot/ module.

3 Cover with compost and firm again gently. The seeds should be covered with about twice their own depth of compost.

4 Stand pots and trays in water until the surface of the compost is moist. Remove from the water and allow to drain.

5 Place in a warm light place. Once the seedlings have come up, gently remove all but the strongest.

Give crops a head start by sowing indoors to plant out when the weather warms up.

Planting out

Once the young plants have at least 4 leaves, and the weather is suitable, they can be planted out, or into larger pots for container growing. Gradually acclimatise the plants to the outside conditions before planting them out. Put the plants outside, still in their original pots or trays, for an increasing period of time each day, for a week or so. This is known as 'hardening off'.

Plant out into moist soil. Dig a small hole for each transplant with a trowel. Use the spacing recommended on the packet. Water well after planting.

What to sow when

Sowing hints and tips

- Check that you are sowing a variety suited to the time of year. Onions, for example, have different varieties for spring and autumn sowing.

- Don't sow when the soil is cold and wet. When the grass begins to grow is soon enough for most hardy crops.

- Sow later on heavy sticky soils as they are slow to warm up.

- The best sowing time will depend on location and the weather conditions.

- Covering the soil with cloches or plastic will warm it up.

- Tomatoes, aubergines and peppers are always raised in pots rather than sowing direct.

- Give tender crops a head start by sowing indoors to plant out when the weather warms up.

Tips for successful all year round veg growing

1 Grow things you like to eat.

2 Plan in advance what you are going to grow where, and when, so you leave space for further sowing and planting.

3 Make several smaller sowings over a period of time .

4 Raise plants in module trays ready to replace those that have finished, or buy plants – especially tomatoes and other tender crops.

5 Harvest crops when young and tender.

6 Check the sowing calendar **on page 44** and plan some later sowings to extend the season.

7 Keep a note of what you grew where, so you don't grow related plants in the same spot every year **(see page 52).**

8 Remove weeds regularly.

9 Check plants frequently and pick off any pests.

What to sow **when**

T* – sow at 15C; do not plant outside until after the last frost.

Vegetable	T*	Sow in trays and pots to transplant	Sowing direct outdoors
Seedling cutting crops		All year round	March - October
Beetroot		February - March	March - June
Broad beans		-	Feb to April
Broccoli – purple sprouting		-	mid April - mid May
Cabbage		February - March	March - May
Calabrese		March - July	April - July
Carrots		-	February - June
Chard and leaf beet		August	March – April; July - early Aug
Chinese cabbage		June - August	June - August
Courgette and pumpkin	T	May - June	June
Chicory, red		-	Late April - August
Endive		April - May	June and early July
Florence fennel		-	May - July
French beans	T	March - July	Late April - late June
Garlic		-	Oct - Nov; February
Kale		-	April - June
Kohl rabi		February	March - August
Leeks		-	March - early May
Lettuce		February - April; September	April - September
Onion sets		-	Mar - April; August
Pak choi		June - August	June - August
Parsnips		-	February - May
Peas		-	March - July
Peppers	T	April – May	-
Potatoes		-	March - May
Radish		-	February - August
Rocket		-	Feb - June; Aug - early Oct
Runner beans	T	April – May	Late May - early July
Spinach		-	Mar - May; August
Spring onions		-	Feb - June; August
Sweetcorn	T	Feb – May	May
Tomatoes, for outdoor growing	T	Late March – early April	-

Growing methods

3

Growing **in beds**

Growing in beds is one of the best ways of growing vegetables – particularly in a garden where space is limited and/or appearance is important.

A vegetable bed is simply an area of ground with a path around it. A **width of 1.2m for the bed** and **30-60cm for the path** works well. The length depends on the available space. If you can fit in at least 4 equal sized beds, this makes crop rotation (page 52) easier to manage. Digging, thinning, weeding etc is done from the path, so beds can be intensively planted, giving high returns from a small area.

Vegetables are grown **evenly spaced** across the bed – the distance between plants being the same in all directions. As a general rule, add the recommended 'between plant' and 'between row' spacing together, then divide the figure by 2 to give the spacing when growing on beds. You can, in some cases, adjust the spacing to give you the size of vegetable you want.

Soil is prepared in the usual way. Once a bed is established there is little need for digging as the soil is not walked on.

For a neat finish, put wooden edging (about 15cm deep) around each bed, and mulch the paths with bark or woodchips.

Vegetables
without digging

It is a myth that growing vegetables is all about hard, heavy digging. In fact there's no need to dig at all!

A 'no dig' approach is good for the soil, as digging only disturbs the established soil structure. 'No dig' cuts down on weeding too as digging encourages weed seeds to germinate.

To go 'no dig' on a new site, prepare the soil as advised on page 24. On an established area, simply stop digging. On a heavy soil it makes sense to combine 'no digging' with a bed system.

Growing in beds is one of the best ways of growing vegetables – particularly in a garden where space is limited and/or appearance is important.

Moisture loving crops may be mulched with leafmould, grass mowings, hay, straw or whatever you have to hand.

'No Dig' **know how**

Soil improvers and fertilisers are spread on the soil surface at the usual rate. The worms do the rest.

Seeds are sown into shallow drills and transplants planted into trowel holes as normal.

Potatoes are grown on the soil surface under a cover of straw or hay (see opposite).

Weeds are removed by hand, hoed off or covered with a light-excluding mulch (a mulch is any organic matter laid on top of the soil) such as newspaper topped with grass mowings.

Runner beans and other moisture loving crops are mulched with leafmould, grass mowings, hay, straw or whatever you have to hand.

Roots crops and leeks are best loosened with a fork before harvest.

No Dig potato growing

Start no dig potatoes in mid April or later, when the soil has really warmed up.

1 Remove, cut down or mow short any weeds or grass on the plot.

2 Water soil well if dry.

3 Spread compost or manure at the normal rate.

4 Plant seed potatoes in shallow trowel holes at the required spacing.

5 Cover the rows with a 10-15cm deep layer of old straw or hay.

6 As the potatoes begin to grow, help the shoots through the straw layer.

7 Add more mulch over the whole area as plants grow.

8 Just before plants meet between the rows, cover the straw or hay mulch with a 7.5cm layer of grass mowings. This helps keep the mulch in place, and to keep light from the developing tubers. Top the grass up where necessary to keep a good cover.

9 To harvest the potatoes, just pull back the mulch and pick the tubers up from the soil surface. You can replace the mulch and allow the rest to continue growing.

Growing in **containers**

Growing vegetables in containers may be the only option if you have a balcony or patio garden. It is also a good method for growing the more tender crops which can only go outside in the height of summer – and for bringing vegetables closer to home.

The **right pot**

The container should have holes in the bottom to allow water to drain out, and it should be at least 15cm deep. Larger containers are easier to look after than small, so it makes sense to grow several small plants together. The bigger the plant, the larger the container.

Some example pot sizes

25cm diameter pot, 30cm deep – 1 potato.

2 gallon bucket (drill holes in the bottom) - 1 courgette.

Window box 15 x 45cm – 4 french beans or 3 looseleaf or compact lettuces.

Polystyrene fish box 30 x 45 x 15cm - 3 rows of early carrots; cutting salad mixes.

Vegetables for pots

Most vegetables will grow well in a container, given the right attention. Those to avoid are large, deep rooted and slow growing crops – such as parsnips, cauliflower, sprouting broccoli. You can crowd the plants a little more than you would in the open ground. Try out different combinations to give a pleasing visual effect.

Filling the pot

Put a layer of gravel, broken up polystyrene or stones in the base of the container.

Fill it with a good quality, peat free, certified organic multipurpose compost. Leave a gap of a few centimetres between the compost and the rim of the pot to make watering easier.

Aftercare

Container grown vegetables do need extra attention. In the height of summer a container may need to be watered twice a day.

Because they are growing in a restricted space, vegetables in containers will need feeding with a liquid fertiliser from around 8 weeks after planting. Use a proprietary certified organic liquid feed, following the instructions on the bottle.

Try to avoid growing vegetables from the same family in the same place more than one year in 3 or 4.

Vegetable **families** and crop **rotation**

Vegetables come in families, and members of the same family tend to be prone to the same pests and diseases.

When growing vegetables try to avoid growing vegetables from the same family in the same place more than one year in 3 or 4. This is known as **crop rotation;** it helps to prevent a build up of soil pests and diseases, and makes best use of the soil fertility. This is one of the most important principles of organic growing - prevention is always better than cure!

Beet family

Beetroot, chard, spinach beet

Cabbage family

Cabbage, kale, brussels sprouts, calabrese, cauliflower, broccoli, pak choi, chinese cabbage, oriental greens, kohl rabi, radish, turnip, swede

Carrot family

Carrot, parsnip, parsley, celery, celeriac

Cucumber family

Cucumber, courgette, pumpkin, squash

Lettuce family

Lettuce, endive, chicory, salsify, scorzonera

Onion family

Onion, leek, garlic, shallots

Pea and bean family

All peas and beans

Potato family

Potato, tomato, pepper and aubergine

action stations

1 **Choose your seeds** and sow direct or in pots or trays.

2 **Buy seed potatoes** and set them in a cool, dry and light spot in egg boxes.

3 **Grow in beds** – you may not even need to dig.

4 **Learn** about vegetable families and crop rotation.

Maintenance

Aftercare

Take time to wander around your vegetable plot every few days. Get to know your plants and you will begin to recognise what is doing well, and what is not so happy.

Weeding

When the vegetable plants are small, keep the soil around them free of weeds. Gently pull out weed seedlings, or hoe them off, when the weeds are still small. If you have sown the seed in rows, you should be able to tell the difference between weed and vegetable seedlings.

Weeding becomes less critical as plants grow larger, but try to keep on top of it. Hand weeding is best done when the soil is moist; hoeing is most effective when the soil is dry. Mulching (see page 58) can help keep weeds down.

Watering

Water seedlings and transplants every few days in dry weather, until they start to grow strongly. Water established plants when they need water, rather than on a regular basis.

In dry spells, water plants in the ground every 10 days or so. Give the ground a thorough soaking of around 15-20 litres per square metre of bed, rather than a light sprinkling which will not penetrate the soil.

Plants in containers may need watering twice a day in hot weather. Vegetables in the soil need little additional water unless there is a prolonged dry spell, or the soil is very quick to drain.

Vegetables that benefit most from watering in dry weather:
Leafy crops such as lettuce, spinach and summer cabbage.
Flowering and fruiting crops, such as tomatoes, courgettes, peas and beans (particularly runner beans) once they start to flower.
Celeriac, celery and florence fennel, should never be allowed to dry out.

Improving the soil with compost and leafmould, and mulching with organic materials reduces the need for watering.

Pinch out the side shoots that develop on tall growing tomato varieties as they appear. DO NOT remove side shoots from bush varieties.

A rich organic mulch helps to keep soil moist, suppress weeds and will slowly feed your plants.

Mulching

Mulching simply means spreading a material out over the soil surface. Mulching the soil helps to keep it moist and suppress weeds, and will gradually improve the structure. A rich mulch such as green waste compost or well rotted manure (see pages 29-30) will also slowly feed the plants.

Grass mowings also make a good short term mulch. Lay sheets of newspaper (several layers thick) on the soil under the mowings for weed control.

For best results, don't mulch until the soil is warm and the plants to be mulched are growing strongly. Never mulch dry soil, as the mulch will tend to keep it dry.

Feeding

Most vegetables grown in the soil, rather than in pots, do not need additional feeding if you have prepared the ground before sowing or planting. Too much feeding can result in excess growth that pests love.

If the soil is not very fertile, plants that are 'greedy feeders' and those that are in the ground for a long time may benefit from a nutrient rich mulch or an organic fertiliser after a month or two.

Plants that are likely to benefit from a rich mulch - tomatoes, leeks, cabbage, brussels sprouts, courgettes.

Some flowers to **attract pest eating insects**

Hoverflies, wasps, ladybirds and flower bugs are some of the insect predators that will help control pests - attract them by planting some of the following near your vegetable patch:

- Cornflower
- Gazania
- Corn marigold
- Sunflower
- Fennel
- Nemophila
- Californian poppy
- Poached egg plant
- Pot marigold
- Annual convolvulus
- French marigolds
- Yarrow

Tips for growing healthy vegetables

1 Don't grow the same veg, or a close relation, in the same place twice in a row. Wait 3-4 years before coming back to that spot.

2 Don't sow or plant too early.

3 Do a regular round of inspection; pick off pests and diseased leaves.

4 Feed the soil with garden compost – proven to help reduce pest and disease problems and nourishes the soil naturally.

5 Grow varieties with some natural resistance.

6 Grow flowers to attract hoverflies, lacewings and other creatures that eat pests.

7 Protect young plants with home-made plastic bottle cloches.

8 If you do need to use a pest spray, choose an organic one, designed for the purpose.

See 'Healthy Plants' and 'Control Pests' in the Green Essentials series for further information.

action stations

1 **Keep an eye on** your veg plants so you can spot any problems early on.

2 **Water plants** in containers every day.

3 **Remove weeds regularly** so plants are not smothered.

4 **Mulch plants** to keep the soil moist and help suppress weeds.

Want more organic gardening help?

Then join HDRA, the national charity for organic gardening, farming and food.

As a member of HDRA you'll gain-
- free access to our Gardening Advisory Service
- access to our three gardens in Warwickshire, Kent and Essex and to 10 more gardens around the UK
- opportunities to attend courses and talks or visit other gardens on Organic Gardens Open Weekends
- discounts when ordering from the Organic Gardening Catalogue
- discounted membership of the Heritage Seed Library
- quarterly magazines full of useful information

You'll also be supporting-
- the conservation of heritage seeds
- an overseas organic advisory service to help small-scale farmers in the tropics
- Duchy Originals HDRA Organic Gardens for Schools
- HDRA Organic Food For All campaign
- research into organic agriculture

To join HDRA ring: 024 7630 3517
email: enquiries@hdra.org.uk
or visit our website: www.hdra.org.uk

Charity No. 298104

Resources

HDRA the organic organisation promoting organic gardening farming and food
www.hdra.org.uk
024 7630 3517

Soil Association the heart of organic food and farming
www.soilassociation.org
0117 929 0661

The HDRA Encyclopedia of Organic Gardening
Dorling Kindersley
editor Pauline Pears

MAIL ORDER:

The Organic Gardening Catalogue
Organic seeds, composts, raised beds, barriers, traps and other organic gardening sundries. All purchases help to fund the HDRA's charity work.
www.organiccatalogue.com
0845 1301304

Garland Products Ltd
Raised beds
www.garlandproducts.com
01384 278256

Rooster – Greenvale Farms Ltd
Chicken manure based fertilisers
www.rooster.uk.com
01677 422953

Suffolk Herbs
Organic vegetable and herb seeds
www.suffolkherbs.com
01376 572456

Tamar Organics
Organic seeds
www.tamarorganics.co.uk
01822 834887

The Wormcast Company
Organic fertiliser
www.thewormcastcompany.com
0845 605 5000

who, what, where, when and why organic?

for all the answers and tempting offers go to www.whyorganic.org

- Mouthwatering offers on organic produce
- Organic places to shop and stay across the UK
- Seasonal recipes from celebrity chefs
- Expert advice on your food and health
- Soil Association food club – join for just £1 a month

Soil Association
the heart of organic food & farming